Lots to See

By Carmel Reilly

Liv sits on a big log.

Kit the cat sits on
the log, too.

Look, Kit! I can see lots!

Liv can see Kev the dog.

Kev got wet in the dam.

Rev the ram runs to the vat.

Rev gets fed.

Kim the kid tugs at the pen.

Liv looks at Lil the red hen.

Lil jabs at bugs and pips.

It is a web.

Can Liv see an ant?

No!

It is **not** an ant on the web!

CHECKING FOR MEANING

1. Who can Liv see? *(Literal)*

2. Where is Kim the kid? *(Literal)*

3. What do you think Rev the ram likes to eat? *(Inferential)*

EXTENDING VOCABULARY

runs	Look at the word *runs*. What is the base of this word? What sound does the *s* on the end make? Find some other words in the book where *s* makes the same sound.
pen	Find a word in the book that rhymes with *pen*. Which of the following letters can you use in front of *–en* to make another word – *t, d, n, s, m*?
jabs	The word *jabs* means "pokes roughly or quickly". How is this word used in the story? Make a sentence of your own using *jabs*.

MOVING BEYOND THE TEXT

1. What can you see in your classroom?

2. What can you see around the school?

3. What are some places where you might see bugs?

4. Where do ants live?

SPEED SOUNDS

Kk	Ll	Vv	Qq	Ww		
Dd	Jj	Oo	Gg	Uu		
Cc	Bb	Rr	Ee	Ff	Hh	Nn
Mm	Ss	Aa	Pp	Ii	Tt	

PRACTICE WORDS

log

Kit

Liv

Rev

Kev

vat

wet

Kim

Lil

kid

lots

web